Mind
Sparklers

Fireworks for Igniting
Creativity in Young Minds

Mind Sparklers

Book 1 for Grades K–3

Robert E. Myers

Prufrock Press
Waco, Texas

ISBN 1-882664-32-9

Prufrock Press
P.O. Box 8813
Waco, TX 76714-8813
(800) 998-2208
e-mail: prufrock@prufrock.com

This volume is dedicated to my mentor, colleague, and longtime friend, E. Paul Torrance, without whose inspiration this and most of what I have produced for the past 36 years, wouldn't exist.

Contents

Contents

A Note to the Teacher

The 40 activities that follow were all designed to persuade your students to think critically and creatively. Some of the activities will appeal to those of your students who enjoy playing with language; others will be more successful with students who enjoy drawing or constructing or singing or moving in various ways.

I have always believed that activities such as these are more effective in encouraging thinking and further learning when teachers modify and adapt them to the personalities, backgrounds, and capabilities of their students. So I urge you to become my co-author. I am sure that the activities will be greatly improved if you accept this invitation.

The theoretical underpinnings for this collection are based upon some philosophical and pedagogical beliefs that are anything but new. For example, I believe, along with many educators, that the experiences are positive—if students can succeed in acquiring knowledge and skills, they can grow intellectually, socially, and emotionally. One of the most effective ways of providing students with opportunities to be successful is to allow them to express their individuality in a psychologically safe environment. In such an environment, they can experiment with ideas that may succeed or fail, and express themselves without fear of being ridiculed.

Setting the stage for these activities is crucial to the success of your students. I hope you will be alert to occasions when the activities tie in with ongoing units of study or topics that have naturally arisen and are of genuine interest to your students. More importantly, I sincerely hope you can prepare and administer these activities in an atmosphere of trust and goodwill. If the activities in this book are presented in a spirit of adventure and of respect for each individual's worth and potentialities, I expect your students to make some progress in academic and personal growth.

I believe that learning is fun and that a sense of humor is indispensable in both teachers and students, but the activities themselves should not be occasions when students think that anything goes—that the wilder their behavior the better. The fun for your students can come from discovering their world while also discovering more and more about themselves. The fun for you can come in witnessing these discoveries.

Tying the Activities to the Curriculum

There are countless ways to introduce units of study in the classroom. Many teachers rely upon curriculum guides to assist them in preparing to teach a topic, and most guides have a wealth of suggestions for bringing in materials that will motivate students to acquire a body of knowledge. What I offer in *Mind Sparklers* is an opportunity to provoke your students to think rather deeply about a topic or an issue. These activities can serve to get your students intellectually and emotionally involved with a subject in a way that a typical guide does not. To be specific, activities in this book are designed to "hook" your students by means of devices such as humor, mysteries, incongruities, games, and puzzles. We think of this approach as one of "coming through the back door."

Although the twin purposes of the activities in *Mind Sparklers* are to encourage independent thinking and to stimulate further learning, they also reinforce the skills and understandings of the regular curriculum. For example, "A Mixed-Up World" deals with the bizarre consequences of some unlikely conditions. One of its zany hypothetical situations concerns the consequences that would occur if all the shoes in the world were the same size. After getting caught up in the humor of that improbability, your pupils should be doing some thinking. The thinking they do sets the stage for the final question of the activity: "What would you like to see change in your town?" My strategy is to get your students' imaginations working and then to present them with a serious question that deals with the social studies topic of the community.

To help you tie the activities to the basic curriculum, we have indicated in the Table of Contents some possible study units in language arts, social studies, mathematics, health, and art.

Torrance's Creative Thinking Abilities

The activities in *Mind Sparklers* call for all 18 of E. Paul Torrance's creative thinking abilities. In many cases, an activity elicits more than one ability, along with the critical thinking skills of analyzing, evaluating, and hypothesizing. Torrance's three books dealing with his Incubation Model of Teaching (Torrance, 1979; Torrance & Safter, 1990; Torrance & Safter, 1997) will provide you with a complete description of the 18 creative abilities listed below.

- Being Sensitive/Finding the Problem (S)

- Producing Alternatives (PA)

- Being Flexible (F)

- Being Original (O)

- Highlighting the Essence (HE)

- Elaborating (E)

- Keeping Open (KO)

- Being Aware of Emotions (AE)

- Putting Ideas into Context (PIC)

- Combining and Synthesizing (CS)

- Visualizing Richly and Colorfully (VRC)

- Enjoying and Using Fantasy (EF)

- Making It Swing, Making It Ring (SR)

- Looking at It Another Way (LAW)

- Visualizing Inside (VI)

- Breaking Through/Extending Boundaries (BT)

- Letting Humor Flow (H)

- Glimpsing Infinity/Orienting to the Future (OF)

You can identify the creative thinking skills called for in the activities by locating the letters for them at the bottom-right of each activity.

Daily Pictures

Every day Ms. Kim has a student hang the day of the week and the date on the wall with two cards. The cards are hung on hooks at the front of the room.

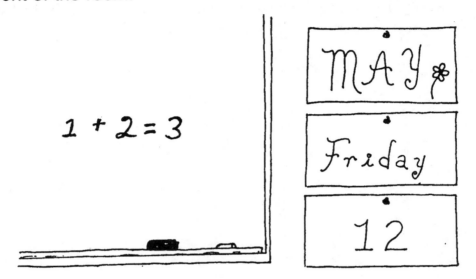

Ms. Kim puts pictures on the top card, which shows the month. She has a picture of a red leaf on the cards of the fall months. She has a picture of a snowflake on the cards of the winter months, and she has a picture of a daisy on the cards of the spring months.

Brenda noticed the daisy on the April card when Missy hung it on the hook. She also saw the daisy when Tom took April off and hung May on the hook. One day she said to Ms. Kim, "I know why you put the daisy on April and May. It's because flowers bloom in the spring."

"That's right, Brenda," Ms. Kim said.

"Why don't you have a picture for each day of the week?" Brenda asked.

"That's a good idea. What pictures should we have for the five school days?" Ms. Kim asked Brenda.

If you were Brenda, what pictures would you ask Ms. Kim to put on the five days of the week? Draw a picture for each day of the week.

Monday

Why did you choose that picture?

_____

Tuesday

Why did you choose that picture?

_____

Wednesday

Why did you choose that picture?

_____

Thursday

Why did you choose that picture?

_____

Friday

Why did you choose that picture?

_____

One *and* One Can Do A Lot!

What is this?   *and*   What is this?

Can you put them together? _____

If you put them together, what can you do with them? _____

_____

_____

What is this?   *and*   What is this?

Can you put them together? _____

If you put them together, what can you do with them? _____

_____

_____

Name: _____

What is this?   *and*   What is this?

   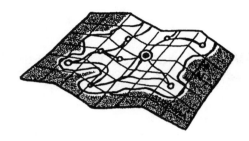

Can you put them together? _____

If you put them together, what can you do with them? _____

_____

_____

What is this?   *and*   What is this?

Can you put them together? _____

If you put them together, what can you do with them? _____

_____

_____

Name:

Chase Challenge

We say that a good joke will chase away gloom, but will gloom chase away a good joke? _____

Why? _____

And what about other things?

1. Does the light chase away the dark, or does the dark chase away the light? _____

   Explain your answer. _____

   _____

   How do you feel when light chases away the dark, or dark chases away the light? _____

   _____

2. Does heat chase away cold, or does cold chase away heat?

_____

Why do you think so?_____

_____

How do you feel when heat chases away cold, or cold chases away heat? _____

_____

3. Does food chase away hunger, or does hunger chase away food?

_____

Explain your answer. _____

_____

What are your feelings when food chases away hunger, or hunger chases away food? _____

_____

4. Does the sun chase away the fog, or does the fog chase away the sun? _____

Why do you think so? _____

_____

When does it happen? _____

_____

5. Does the wind chase away a cloud, or does a cloud chase away the wind? _____

   Why do you think so? _____

   _____

   When does it happen? _____

   _____

6. Does sound chase away silence, or does silence chase away sound? _____

   Why do you think so? _____

   _____

   How do you feel when sound chases away silence, or silence chases away sound? _____

   _____

7. Does a frown chase away a grin, or does a grin chase away a frown? _____

   Explain your answer? _____

   _____

   How do you feel when a frown chases away a grin, or a grin chases away a frown? _____

   _____

Why don't you write a little poem about how you feel when one of those things happens? You could write a cinquain. Cinquains are short, five-line poems, and they aren't hard to write. Here is an example of a cinquain:

Rain	(First line—one word, subject of your poem)
Water drops	(Second line—two words describing subject)
Sprinkling and pouring	(Third line—three words expressing action)
Makes me feel depressed	(Fourth line—four words expressing feelings)
Wet	(Fifth line—another word for the subject)

If you wish, you can disguise the subject in your cinquain and reveal it as a surprise in the last line. As you see, the lines do not rhyme.

There is another way of writing cinquains, using syllables instead of words. The pattern is 2, 4, 6, 8, and 2.

Raindrops
Liquid and sun
Falling and splattering
Makes me feel lonely and depressed—
I'm drenched!

What Would You Do?

What would you do if you saw a turtle in your boot? _____

_____

_____

_____

What would you do if you saw a fox on your roof? _____

_____

_____

_____

What would you do if you saw a penguin in your bed? _____

_____

_____

_____

What would you do if you saw
the tracks of an elephant
behind your house? _____

_____

_____

_____

What would you do if you saw a
frog swimming in your tub? _____

_____

_____

_____

What would be the first thing you would
do if you saw a parrot reading a newspaper?_____

_____

Why? _____

What would be the second thing you would do? _____

_____

Why? _____

Mail

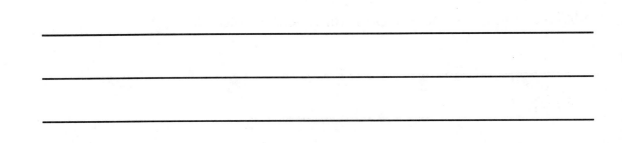

What do you like to find in your mailbox?

_____

A letter from a friend?

_____

A letter from a relative?

_____

A package? _____

There are many things that can come to your mailbox.

Every day, the mail carrier delivers the mail at two o'clock. One Monday, you go to get the mail a little after two o'clock, but the mailbox is empty. You are expecting some mail, and so you go back to the mailbox at three o'clock. It is still empty. What are some of the reasons why the mail is not there? List all you can think of.

_____

_____

_____

_____

Tom's Pickles

"Tom, would you get a jar of pickles from the basement for me?" his mother asked. Tom turned on the lights at the top of the stairs.

After he took a few steps, Tom felt something touch his face ... What was it? _____

_____

_____

When Tom reached the basement, he heard a sound. Then he heard the sound again ... What was it? _____

_____

_____

Finally, he found the jar of pickles. It was on the shelf, right where his mother said it would be. He started to go up the stairs, then he froze. A smile came across his face as he looked in the corner ... What did he see? _____

_____

_____

"Here, Mom," Tom said as he handed her the jar of pickles. "Thanks, dear," his mother said as she gave him a big hug.

Four

What do you think of when you see ...

... a seal? _____

_____

... a woman making music? _____

_____

... a man working in a garden?

_____

_____

... lightning? _____

_____

How are the seal, the woman making music, the man working in the garden, and the lightning different? _____

_____

_____

_____

Are they alike in any way? If so, how are they alike? _____

_____

_____

Look at It Another Way

Although we seem to like some things and not others, there is usually something to like about everything. For example, snow comes in cold weather, but many people enjoy skiing on the snow. Here are some events you may not enjoy. Let's see if you can think of why they might not be so bad.

1. What is the best thing about having a broken arm? _____

_____

2. What do you like about burnt toast? _____

_____

3. What do you like best about a very dark night? _____

_____

4. What do you like best about a rain storm? _____

_____

5. What is the nicest thing about an earthquake? _____

_____

6. What is the best thing about losing a toy? _____

_____

7. What is the best thing about a forest fire? _____

_____

Using one of these situations, show in a drawing why it is a good thing. Use the space below.

A Mixed-Up World

In this activity, you are asked to imagine the changes that would happen if the traits of certain things were changed. Write all of the changes that would take place if these things happened.

1. What could happen if every flower in the world were yellow?

   _____

2. What could happen if peas tasted like candy? _____

   _____

3. What could happen if cows had manes like lions do? _____

   _____

4. What could happen if cats suddenly learned to bark? _____

   _____

5. What could happen if all the shoes in the world were the same size? _____

   _____

   _____

Draw a picture of what might happen if one of these things changed.

What would you like to see change in your town? _____

_____

_____

Why would you like to see it change? _____

_____

_____

Your Magic Pencil

Do you have a magic pencil? When you write with a certain pencil, do you come up with some of your best ideas? Does one pencil feel good in your hand when you use it? Why don't you try out your pencils right now? Gather up all of the pencils near you. Call one of them "Pencil 1" and another "Pencil 2" and so on.

Now write your name with each pencil.

Pencil 1 _____

Pencil 2 _____

Pencil 3 _____

Pencil 4 _____

Which pencil worked best? _____

_____

Let's see what happens when you answer a question that will stretch your mind a little. Which pencil will write the best answer? Write an answer with each pencil, but don't write the same answer twice.

What is a good name for a pet porcupine?

Pencil 1 _____

Pencil 2 _____

Pencil 3 _____

Pencil 4 _____

Which answer do you like best? _____

_____

Was the pencil that wrote the best answer also the one that did the best job of writing your name? _____

If it was, you have found your "magic" pencil.

Draw a picture of the pet porcupine with your magic pencil.

Purple, Not Yellow

Look around you. Do you see anything that is yellow? _____

What is it? _____

_____

Can you imagine that it is purple? _____

_____

What if it *were* purple? _____

_____

_____

Look around you once more. Do you see anything that is green?

_____

What is it? _____

_____

Can you imagine that it is red? _____

_____

What if it *were* red? _____

_____

Now, take another look. Do you see anything that is brown?

_____

What is it? _____

_____

Can you imagine that it is blue? _____

_____

What if it *were* blue? _____

_____

_____

What is your favorite color? _____

_____

Do you think it will always be your favorite color? _____

_____

What would you do if you were told you couldn't wear clothes of that color? _____

_____

_____

_____

_____

Name:

"Sounding" You Out

What sound makes you sleepy? _____

Why does it make you sleepy? _____

Does it make you sleepy every time you hear it? _____

Why? _____

Does the sound make anyone else sleepy? _____

Why? _____

What sound makes you happy when you hear it? _____

Why does it make you happy? _____

_____

Do you hear it every day? _____

When do you hear it most often? _____

Does the sound usually make other boys and girls happy, too?

_____

Why? _____

What sounds make you excited when you hear them? _____

_____

Which of these is the sound you like best? _____

_____

Why? _____

_____

Will you hear the sound often when you grow up? _____

Why? _____

_____

What is a sound? _____

_____

When you are a teenager and you hear these sounds, will you feel the same way? _____

_____

Explain your answer. _____

_____

When you hear these same sounds as an adult, will you feel differently from the way you did as a teenager? _____

_____

Explain your answer. _____

_____

Edna

Nora has a problem. Her little sister Edna is a pest, or so Nora thinks. Every time Nora wants to do something, Edna has to do it, too. If Nora gets a bike, Edna has to ride it, even though she is too small for it. When Nora has a friend over to the house, Edna has to play with them.

It's not much fun having a little sister like Edna, Nora thinks. Their mother wants them both to be happy and get along. Nora wants to get along without Edna.

Maybe you know someone like Edna. Can anything be done so that Nora and Edna are both happy? Is there something that is missing in what goes on between them? Can something be added?

_____

_____

_____

_____

_____

_____

_____

_____

Name:

_____

_____

_____

_____

_____

_____

_____

_____

_____

_____

_____

_____

_____

_____

_____

Which Ball Do You Want?

1. Let's suppose that you want to buy a ball—maybe a big beach ball?

   If you went to a store that sells beach balls, which one would you pick? Would you pick one because of its color? Would you find out the prices of the balls? Would you want one with stripes? Would you see what it was made of? What would be the most important thing to you about the ball? _____

   _____

   _____

2. Now, let's suppose that you do not have much money. If all the balls cost too much, what would you do? _____

   _____

   What if the store didn't have the color you liked? What would you do? _____

   _____

If none of the balls had stripes and you wanted a ball with stripes, what would you do? _____

_____

If all the balls were made of a thin plastic and didn't look like they would last very long, what would you do? _____

_____

3. Would you like to write a story about a ball that someone buys? You could draw a picture of what happens to the ball.

_____

_____

_____

_____

_____

Birds

1. Here is a bird.
Have you ever seen a bird like this? _____

_____

Would you ever expect to see one? _____

_____

Even in your dreams? _____

_____

Do you think it is a friendly bird? _____

_____

Why or why not? _____

_____

Do you think it is a fast flier? _____

_____

Why or why not? _____

_____

Do you think it is a pretty bird? _____

_____

Why or why not? _____

_____

What would be a good name for this bird? _____

2. Here is another bird.
   Have you ever seen one like it? _____

_____

If so, where? _____

Will you ever see one? _____

Where? _____

What do you think it likes to eat? _____

_____

Do you think it is a nice bird? _____

_____

Why or why not? _____

_____

Do you think it is a grumpy bird?_____

Why or why not? _____

_____

How would this bird feel if it saw a bird like the first one? _____

_____

What name would fit this bird? _____

C. Here is a third bird.
What would be a good
name for this bird?

_____

What do you think this bird
likes to do? _____

_____

Which of the three birds do you like best? _____

Why? _____

_____

Would you like to write a story about one of the birds? _____

Which one? _____

You could even write a story about all three of the birds. Use the
space below to write your own story about the three birds.

_____

_____

_____

_____

_____

_____

_____

_____

_____

_____

_____

_____

_____

A Lucky Boy

Gary lives with his father and mother in a gray house. He and his brother Tim sleep in the same room. They each have a bed. Gary is seven and Tim is four.

One rainy Monday, Mrs. Gomez picked up Gary and Hal and took them to school in her car. When it rained, three of the mothers in the neighborhood took turns driving the children to school.

As the children stepped out of the car, Hal put up his umbrella. He asked the other two children if they wanted to get under it. Mary, Gary, and Hal did not get wet when they crossed the street to enter the school.

When it was lunch time, Gary could not find his lunch box. He had left it at home.

His friend Mario gave Gary half an apple and part of his sandwich. Gary thanked Mario, and after lunch they played tag in the school yard. It had stopped raining.

How many examples of sharing are there in this story about Gary? _____

Name each one. _____

_____

_____

Who was the lucky boy in the story? _____

Why? _____

Can you write a short story that has at least two examples of sharing in it? Write it below.

_____

_____

_____

_____

_____

Do you like to share? _____

Why or why not? _____

_____

Why do we share? _____

_____

The Big Red Truck

One day, Hal, Margy, and their father were driving to town. On the way, Hal's father asked Hal what he wanted to be when he grew up.

Hal said, "I want to be a truck when I grow up."

Margy laughed. She was five, and Hal was only three.

Hal's father asked, "What kind of truck do you want to be?"

"A big truck," Hal said.

"What color do you want to be?" Hal's father asked.

"Red," Hal said.

"You would make a good truck, Hal," Margy said.

Did you ever want to be a truck or a car or an airplane? _____

_____

Did you ever want to be something that moves but is not really alive? _____

Let's pretend. Which of these things would you like to be?

a wagon	the moon	a fire engine
a lighthouse	an elevator	a bike
a rocket	a boat	an airplane
a car	a kite	a stove
a train	a camera	the wind

Write the name of the one you would like to be. _____

What color would you be? _____

How big would you be? _____

What would you be doing? _____

Sometimes it's fun to pretend that you are a rocket or the wind.
But you can never really be anything but a person. How is a person different from the wind or a car or a truck? _____

_____

_____

_____

_____

Why is it good to be a person? _____

_____

_____

_____

_____

_____

_____

_____

A City of Animals

Write the name of each animal in its box.

Suppose these animals had their own city. Which one would be the police officer? _____

Why would that animal be a good police officer? _____

_____

How would that animal keep law and order? _____

_____

Which animal would be the firefighter? _____

_____

Why would it be a good firefighter? _____

_____

How would it put out fires? _____

_____

Which animal would be the letter carrier? _____

_____

Why would it be a good letter carrier? _____

_____

How would it deliver the mail? _____

_____

Which one would be the street cleaner? _____

_____

Why would it be a good street cleaner? _____

_____

How would it clean the street? _____

_____

Which animal would be the dentist? _____

_____

Why would it be a good dentist? _____

_____

How would it pull teeth? _____

_____

Which animal would be the bus driver? _____

_____

Why would it be a good bus driver? _____

_____

How would it carry the other animals? _____

_____

Which animal would be the teacher? _____

_____

Why would it be a good teacher? _____

_____

How would it teach the other animals? _____

_____

Which animal would be the mayor? _____

_____

Why would it be a good mayor? _____

_____

How would it govern, rule, and serve the city of animals? _____

_____

What problems would the animals have in their city that we have in our cities? _____

_____

_____

What problems would the animals have in their city that our cities don't have? _____

_____

_____

What problems do our cities have that the animals wouldn't have?

_____

_____

What would be a good name for the animals' city? _____

_____

What games do you like to play? _____

_____

What game do you like best? _____

Would any of the animals in the city of animals like to play the game you like most? _____

_____

If so, which ones? _____

_____

What game do you play that a monkey would like to play? _____

_____

What game do you play that an elephant would like to play? _____

_____

What game do you play that a parrot would like to play? _____

_____

What game do you play that a crocodile would like to play? _____

_____

What game do you play that a snake would like to play? _____

_____

What game do you play that a hippo would like to play? _____

_____

Could any of the animals play a game with a balloon? _____

_____

If so, which ones could play a game with a balloon? _____

_____

Why? _____

_____

_____

In the space below or on a separate sheet of paper, draw a map of the city of animals. Show where the animals live, shop, and go to have fun.

Is Seeing Believing?

When Jim came back to school after summer vacation, he said he had been in China for two months. Peggy told Jim that she did not believe he had gone to China. Jim said that he would prove he had been to China the next day. When he came to school the next day, he showed Peggy some chopsticks. "That proves I've been to China!" Jim shouted.

Did the chopsticks prove that Jim had gone to China? _____

_____

Why or why not? _____

_____

_____

Mary likes to dance. She takes tap dancing lessons every Monday. But Mary did not have many friends. One day Mary told Jane that she had won first prize in a contest. Penny asked Mary to show them her prize. Mary said that she would show them the cup she had won if her mother would let her bring it to school. A few days later, Mary brought a cup and told the girls it was her prize.

Could the cup be proof that Mary had won the prize? _____

_____

How? _____

_____

Mario was one of the biggest boys in his second grade class. He liked to tell everyone how strong he was. One morning he told the boys who sat near him that he could do 15 push-ups. No one said anything. In a louder voice, Mario said that he could do 20 push-ups.

"Go ahead, Mario. Show us," Jack said.

What do you think Mario did? _____

_____

What is the only way that Mario could prove that he could do 20 push-ups? _____

_____

How many ways can you prove something? Write as many as you can think of below.

_____

_____

_____

_____

_____

_____

_____

_____

What Follows?

From what has happened to us before, we know that one event usually follows another. We know that night follows day and Monday follows Sunday.

Below are a number of events. Can you think of what comes after each of them? What comes after ...

... a bump on the head? _____

Why? _____

_____

... a fall into a pond? _____

Why? _____

_____

... knocking over a lamp? _____

Why? _____

_____

... eating too much candy? _____

Why? _____

_____

... finding a dime? _____

Why? _____

_____

... a game of hide-and-seek? _____

Why? _____

_____

Can a fall into a pond come after a bump on the head? _____

When can it happen? _____

_____

Can eating too much candy come after knocking over the lamp?

_____

When can it happen? _____

_____

Can a game of hide-and-seek come after finding a dime? _____

When can it happen? _____

_____

Take one of these events and make a picture of it. You can draw the picture, or cut out pictures in old magazines and paste them on a piece of paper. Have your picture tell what happened next.

Would You Like It?

We become used to seeing people look the same every day. Now and then a person does not wear what you might expect him or her to wear. But usually we are not surprised by the way others look and act. What if some of them decided to change their looks?

Would you like it if the police didn't wear uniforms? _____

Why or why not? _____

_____

Would you like it if librarians did wear uniforms? _____

Why or why not? _____

_____

Would you like it if every teacher at your school wore a flower to school? _____

Why or why not? _____

_____

Would you like it if all of the mail carriers in your neighborhood used inline skates? _____

Why or why not? _____

_____

Would you like it if newspaper carriers were all over 60 years old?

_____

Why or why not? _____

_____

Would you like it if the mayor of your city was also the city's dog catcher? _____

Why or why not? _____

_____

Draw a picture of one of these workers. Show what he or she would look like. Show the person at work. Be sure to use crayons or colored pencils and have lots of colors in your picture.

Name:

A Quarter Is Enough

Jill and her mother went to the grocery store to buy some groceries. While they were there, Jill saw some candy.

"May I have a bag of those gum drops, Mom?" she asked.

"I'm not sure, Jill. I may not have enough money to buy all of our groceries and the candy, too," her mother said.

Jill loved gum drops, and she wanted them very much. "OK, Mom," she said.

When they finished putting all of the groceries into their cart, Jill's mother looked into her purse. "There may be enough money left over," she said. "I have $16."

"If you don't have enough, I may have a little money to help buy the candy," Jill said. She looked into her little purse and found a quarter. "Oh, I have a quarter."

The total bill for the groceries was $15.35. Jill's bag of candy cost $.85. Jill's mother told her, "If you can figure out how much more money we need for the candy, you may have it. How much money will you have to give to me?"

 Do you think that Jill figured out how much she had to give her mother? _____

How much money did Jill have to give her mother to get the candy? _____

Did Jill figure better or worse because she wanted the candy so much? _____

_____

Tell why. _____

_____

_____

Some people aren't able to do math when they get excited. Sometimes, they get mixed up. Are you that way?

Family Figures

Some people think of figures such as 1, 2, and 3 as being a little like people. For example, one person might imagine 8 to be like a mother and 4 to be like a son. Have you ever thought about figures being like people in some way? Let's see if you can do that kind of imagining.

If 8 is the mother and 4 is the son, what is 2? _____

_____

If 9 is the father and 3 is the daughter, what is 6? _____

_____

If 5 is the son and 10 is the father, what is 15? _____

_____

If 13 is the aunt and 14 is the uncle, what is 12? _____

_____

Would you rather live next door to 8, 4, and 2, or 9, 3, and 6? ___

_____

Why? _____

_____

Even Numbers

 ENOUGH

 E-N-U-F-F ENUFF

Mr. Toy divided his class into two groups of the same number. He wanted the children to have a spelling bee. The two groups had to have the same number of children. If they didn't, it wouldn't be fair. Why? _____

_____

What could Mr. Toy do if he had 15 children in his class? _____

_____

In games, when do you want even sides?

In tag? _____

In dodge ball? _____

In jacks? _____

In relay races? _____

Do you want even sides when you go fishing? _____

Why or why not? _____

_____

Check

It was the first day of school. Tina had asked her father to put her school things in a bag. When she got to school, she opened the bag. She found three erasers and a pencil. Tina laughed out loud.

When she came home that afternoon, Tina's father met her at the door.

"How did it go, Tina?" her father asked.

"Fine," Tina said, "except I had three erasers and one pencil."

"Oh, I'm sorry, dear," Tina's father said. "I must have gotten mixed up. You wanted three pencils and one eraser, didn't you? I should have checked your bag before you left to see if it was right."

The next day, Tina's teacher, Ms. Gomez, gave this problem to the class:

$$\begin{array}{r} 14 \\ -\ 8 \\ \hline \end{array}$$

Tina put down 5 as her answer.

Ms. Gomez said to her class, "You can check to see if your answer is right. It's always a good idea to check your answer. Just take your answer and add it to 8. If you have 14, you are right."

Tina added 5 and 8 and got 13. She knew her answer was wrong.

What is the right answer? _____

What did Tina learn during the first two days of school? How could she use what she learned at home or in society? _____

_____

_____

Look Again

How many triangles do you see here?

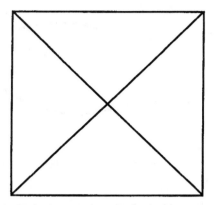

Do you see four triangles? _____

Can you see more than four triangles? _____

Can you see six different triangles? _____

Can you see eight different triangles? _____

Look at a button on your clothes. How many circles
do you see?

Can you see three circles? _____

Can you see more than that? _____

How many can you see? _____

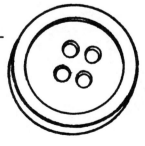

Tops and Bottoms

What is this the bottom of? _____

What is this a top of? _____

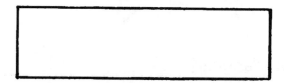

What is this the side of? _____

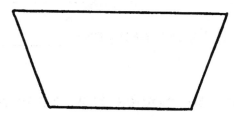

Draw some more of it.

Name: _____

What is this the top of? _____

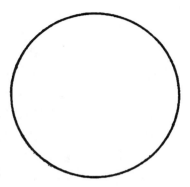

What is this the side of?

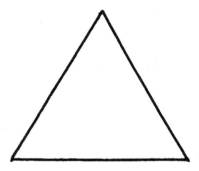

Draw some more of it.

Four Hearts

Maria wanted to make four valentines. She only had one piece of red paper. And, she had a big heart made of cardboard. She thought she could trace the heart on the red paper, then she could cut it out.

The red paper is the same size as her writing paper—8½ inches wide and 11 inches long. She found that her cardboard heart was 4½ inches wide and 5 inches long. That was more than half as wide as her red paper. If she traced the heart on the red paper, she couldn't cut out two, side by side.

Maria doesn't want to try to make a smaller heart out of the cardboard. She likes the one she has. She thinks she can find some way to get four hearts cut from the red paper.

Is Maria right?
Can she cut four hearts, 4½ inches wide and 5 inches long, out of the red piece of paper?
Try it. Use the heart on the next page.

(We think Maria did it.)

Name:

Three Flags

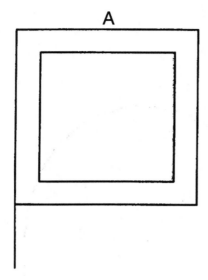

A

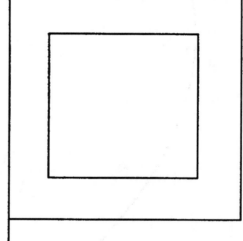

B

Which flag is the largest?

_____

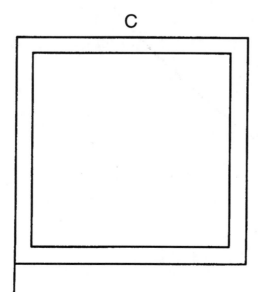

C

Which is the smallest?

_____

How can you tell which flag is largest and which is smallest? Use a ruler, a piece of string, or a piece of paper to see if you were right. Were you right? _____

_____

If you were not right, can you guess why?_____

_____

Sometimes things aren't the way they seem to be. Mountains can seem to be larger or smaller than they really are. What other things have not been what you thought they were? _____

_____

_____

Do you know why you were fooled by any of these things?

_____

_____

_____

_____

_____

_____

_____

_____

A Bat in a Hat

A bat has warm blood.
A bat's babies are born alive.
A bat has hair on its body.
In these ways a bat is like a human.

A bat has wings and it flies.
Most bats eat a lot of insects.
Most bats live in dark places like caves and sleep upside down.
In these ways a bat is *not* like a human.

Which would you rather be—a bat or a human—if you were ...

... in a hat? _____

Why? _____

... in a wind storm? _____

Why? _____

... at the North Pole? _____

Why? _____

... on a hot desert? _____

Why? _____

... at a ball game? _____

Why? _____

... at a movie? _____

Why? _____

... in a car? _____

Why? _____

... on an island with just fruit trees on it? _____

Why? _____

Turnabout

Can you imagine what might happen if rabbits were as slow as snails? _____

_____

_____

Or, if snails were as ferocious as tigers? _____

_____

_____

Or, if tigers were as playful as monkeys? _____

_____

_____

Or, if monkeys were as quiet as mice? _____

_____

_____

Or, if mice were as strong as horses?

_____

_____

Or, if horses were as noisy as turkeys? _____

_____

_____

Or, if turkeys were as slippery as eels? _____

_____

_____

Or, if rabbits were as _____

as _____ ?

Would a snail really be a snail if it were *fast* or if it were *ferocious*? _____

_____

Explain your answer. _____

_____

_____

Have you had any ideas about pets or other animals? _____

_____

_____

_____

Kings and Queens

We call the lion the "King of Beasts." When you hear the lion called that, you get the idea that he bosses the other animals around. Except for the elephant and a few others, that is true.

Have you thought about giving royal names to other animals? It seems right that some other animals should have names that suit their size, strength, and brains.

Which fish should be called the "King of the Fishes"? _____

_____

Why? _____

Which insect should be called the "Queen of the Insects"? _____

_____

Why? _____

Which bird should be called "Princess of the Birds"? _____

_____

Why? _____

Which reptile should be called "Prince of the Reptiles"? _____

_____

Why? _____

Draw the Animal

Here is an animal that has never been seen by anyone. There may be one some place, or there may not be one.

It has six long red legs.
It has two big blue wings.
It can swim.
It has a long stinger.
It has six eyes.
It has yellow horns.

Draw a picture of the animal. Use crayons or watercolors to color it in after you have drawn it in pencil.

Changing

Mr. Burns was talking about an idea in science class. The idea was that every living thing changes. He talked about animals changing and the chick that had hatched from an egg in class last week. Mr. Burns talked about trees growing from seedlings to giant trees. He talked about tiny things changing, such as little animals of only one cell breaking in two and becoming two animals.

"Everything changes all the time," he said, "and nothing stays the same."

"Nothing *ever* stays the same?" James asked.

"No. In fact, you are different today than you were yesterday."

"I feel the same," James said.

"Yes, but you are slightly different. You may weigh one or two ounces more," Mr. Burns said. "Your hair is a tiny bit longer. You are just a little different."

When James went home, he thought about what Mr. Burns had said. He had said that some changes come fast, as when a tadpole becomes a frog. But other things take a long time. James looked around and wondered. He guessed that even things that weren't alive changed. His father had said that the house would need painting in a year. It had been painted two years ago. If you looked closely, you could see flakes of paint on the side of the house.

Was his dog different today? Speedy was still a puppy. He would get bigger and stronger, but James knew that dogs get old. He had seen Ben, his brother's dog, get old and lame. James hoped that Speedy wouldn't get lame. He went to the kitchen and found a carrot and ate it. James wondered if carrots change.

Do carrots change? _____

How do they change? _____

Would eating that carrot change James? _____

How would eating a carrot change James? _____

_____

_____

Would eating a mashed carrot change James more than it would change a baby? _____

_____

Why do you think so? _____

_____

_____

_____

_____

Take It Apart

If you take this apart, what will you have? _____

What can you do with the parts?

_____

If you take this apart, what will you have? _____

What can you do with the parts?

_____

If you take this apart, what will you have? _____

What can you do with the parts?

_____

If you take this apart, what will you have? _____

What can you do with the parts?

_____

If you take this apart, what will you have? _____

What can you do with the parts?

_____

If you take this apart, what will you have? _____

What can you do with the parts?

_____

If you take this apart, what will you have? _____

What can you do with the parts?

_____

Airborne

What would you rather be—a raindrop or a kite? _____

Why? _____

_____

What does a raindrop do? _____

Can a kite do the same things? _____

Would you like to be a raindrop in the summer?

_____

In the winter? _____

In the spring? _____

On a mountain top?

_____

On an island? _____

_____

Name: _____

What would you see in the daytime?

_____

What would you see at night? _____

_____

Show how you would be a raindrop or a kite by ...

... dancing like one.

... by singing about what would happen to you if you were one.

... by drawing what you think would happen to you if you were one.

... by writing about what you would do if you were a raindrop or a kite. _____

_____

_____

_____

This and That

Why is a horn like a bell? _____

_____

Why is a helicopter like a balloon? _____

_____

Why is a ship like a house? _____

_____

Why is a zoo like a city? _____

_____

Why is a whale like a whistle? _____

_____

Why is a jar of jam like a hat? _____

_____

Why is a pan like a hammer? _____

_____

Sue Swings

Sue was four years old. In the fall, she and her family moved to a new house. One day, Sue's father went to the store and bought some rope and wood. When he came home, he tied both ends of the rope to a limb of the oak tree in the yard. Then he cut the board, put notches on the sides, and placed it on the loop that the rope made.

"Sue, would you like to try out our new swing?" her father asked.

"No, thank you, Daddy," Sue answered.

A few days later, Sue's mother asked her if she wanted to go out and swing.

"I don't think so," Sue said. "I tried to swing at Nancy's one time and I fell off."

"All right," Sue's mother said.

Several months later in the spring, Sue was playing in the yard with her friend Carol. Carol was five. She was swinging while Sue sat under the oak tree with her doll.

"Would you like to swing now?" Carol asked.

"OK," Sue said.

Sue got on the seat of the swing and began to go back and forth a little.

"Push your legs to the front and pull back on the ropes," Carol said.

Sue did as Carol told her. Soon she was swinging.

"This is fun!" Sue laughed.

Sue's father had his own way of making a swing. Do you know another way to make a swing? _____

Draw a picture below showing how *you* would make a swing.

Why didn't Sue want to swing at first? _____

_____

Do you know why she decided to swing several months later?

_____

Did you have trouble when you first tried to ride a bike? _____

What happened? _____

_____

Were you able to skip rope the first time you tried? _____

If not, how long did it take before you could do it? _____

_____

Have you ever had trouble learning to do something? _____

What was it? _____

Out of Place

Which animal shouldn't be where it is? Circle it.

Which animal is out of place? Circle it.

Which person should be some place else? Circle it.

Now look at the three things you circled. What can you put in their places? On a separate sheet of paper, draw three pictures and paste them over the things that don't fit.

Now, draw a picture of three or four people. Draw one person that doesn't fit with the others.

Why is one of the people in your drawing out of place? _____

_____

What Will Happen?

What is going to happen?

Draw what happened below.

References

Torrance, E.P. (1979) *The Search for Satori and Creativity.* Buffalo, NY: Creative Education Foundation.

Torrance, E.P. & Safter, H.T. (1990). *The Incubation Model of Teaching.* Buffalo, NY: Bearly Limited.

Torrance, E.P. & Safter, H.T. (1997). *Making the Creative Leap Beyond.* Buffalo, NY: Bearly Limited.